Life Without My Mummy?

By Romeo Bremmer, Aged 7

Life Without My Mummy?

A BlackJac Media Book
First paperback and Hardback edition printed in 2015 in the United Kingdom

Copyright © 2015 Romeo Bremmer. All rights reserved.

Text: Romeo Bremmer with Yazmin McKenzie
All Selfies: Romeo Bremmer
Cover Photograph: Yazmin McKenzie
Back Cover and P13 Photograph: Jak Flash
Romeo SCBU Photograph: Homerton Hospital Midwife Team
Romeo in Egypt Photograph: Lyz Bailey

Design: Andy Pryor
Artworker: Becky Wybrow
Sub Editor: Jackie Raymond

A CIP catalogue record of this book is available from the British Library.
ISBN (PBK) 9780993316814
ISBN (HBK) 9780993316807
ISBN (eBook-ePub) 9780993316821
ISBN (AUDIO) 9780993316838

All rights reserved.
No part of this publication may be reproduced, stored in a retrieval system, or transmitted, in any form, or by any means, electrical, mechanical, photocopying, recording, or otherwise without the prior permission of the publisher.

For orders or enquiries contact: BlackJac Media
Telephone: 07429481305
www.blackjacmedia.com

Printed by Bailey McKenzie

For my Mummy, Nanny Yaz, Bails, Grandad Ken & Aunty Lyz

Because I love you all more than Lego.

Love Romeo x

My name is Romeo Benson Isaiah Bremmer and I'm 7 years old.

I live in Hackney in East London *with my Mummy Juliet, my sister Yazmin, my brother Bailey, my dog K-9 and my cat Chardonnay.*

My dad used to live with us but, when I was two, my Mummy and Dad divorced. Dad would come and see me every month and bring me toys, like Ben10 and Lego. One month, he just stopped visiting and I never saw him again.

I was sad because I really liked spending time with him. Then I felt angry. I was so angry I wanted to change my surname from Bremmer to Jackson. I changed my mind after Granddad Ken began to pick me up every other Saturday. I would stay at his house with Grandma Dell. My granddad is great. He used to drive a bus but is retired. We go to the park, shopping in Westfields and ride on the buses and trains.

Sometimes, we visit my big cousins L'wren, Lance and Rhian, who is a dancer and was a finalist in the television programme, 'Britain's Got Talent'.

I have lots of fun with my family. My sister Yaz takes me to the cinema to watch the latest movie releases.

My brother Bailey works in a bank and gives me £10 pocket money every week; Uncle Kevin and I go to museums and the library, and Aunty Lyz takes me to the theatre to watch plays and pantomimes. Every week, my Mummy and I go to swimming lessons and football training.

We go on holiday a lot, too. I have been to Jamaica, Florida, Egypt, Greece, Tunisia, France, Malta and Spain. One of the best places my Mummy has taken me to is Legoland in Windsor. We went on May 4th and it was a special *Star Wars* day. It was amazing, because Stars Wars is my favourite movie. I have seen all the episodes from 1 to 6. I did Jedi training and met the characters Darth Vader, Darth Maul and Boba Fett, and watched Anakin, Princess Leia and the Storm Troopers in the parade. I have also been to the Secret Cinema presents *Star Wars* and the New *Star Wars* Experience at Madame Tussauds, the waxworks museum in Baker Street. I went with Uncle Peter, who loves *Star Wars* even more than I do. The Jedi Master, Qui-Gon Jinn, looked like a real person.

I love playing with Lego, because I like construction and building things. It's my favourite toy in the world. I always follow the instructions on the booklet, and build exactly what it looks like on the box. After, I like to break it all up and make something else using my imagination.

My hobbies are swimming - I'm level 2 - and football. I have four trophies and medals. Everyone in my family supports Tottenham Hotspur Football Club. When I was younger, I wanted to support Arsenal, but my Mummy said 'No way'. Every season she buys me the latest Spurs kit. I've been inside the stadium and sat on the manager's leather chair at White Hart Lane, which was really cool.

My Mummy is a senior deputy head teacher in a secondary school. She has a lot of responsibility.

She wants me to be a Cardiologist when I'm older but **I want to be a footballer, a Jedi or an architect.**

My Nanny Lilly lives 10 minutes from our house and takes me to school every morning.

She also picks me up from school, and I sleep at her house every Wednesday night. She was born in Jamaica and has silver hair.

She is a very good cook, and makes lovely cornmeal porridge for breakfast, or ackee and saltfish with tasty fried dumplings. My nan has a massive garden, and is always watering and planting new flowers. She also grows pumpkin, potatoes and tomatoes.

Every morning she wakes up at 6 O'clock and prays with my Godmother Aunty Carmen for all my family and friends.

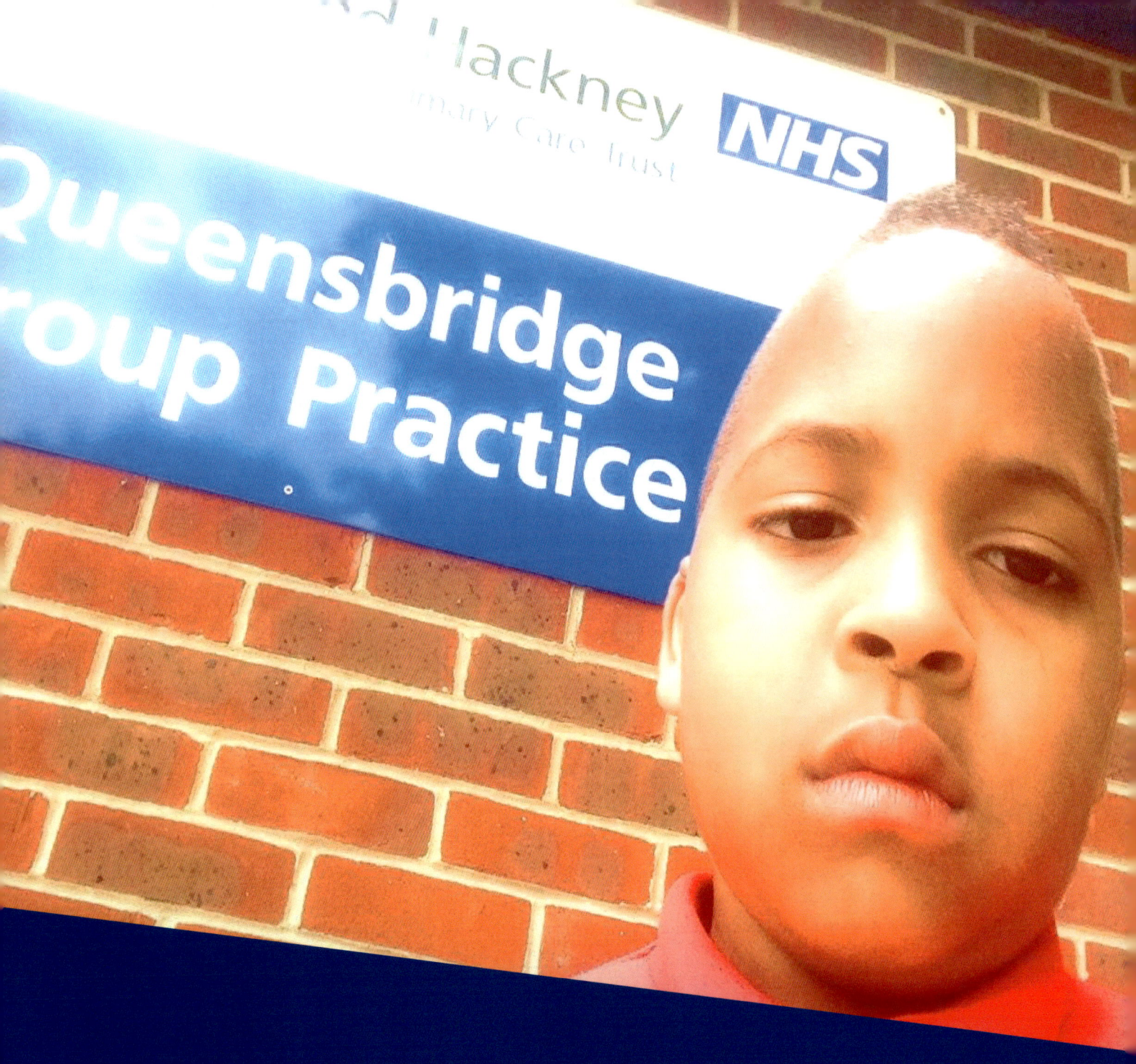

When I was 5 years old something bad happened. My mummy had a heart attack.

She was in hospital for a week having lots of tests. I had heard about heart attacks on the News and that people who had them died. I wasn't allowed to go to the hospital and had nightmares and was very scared and upset. When Mummy was discharged from hospital she had to see her GP Dr Pilkington every week to make sure she was getting better. I would go with her and watch the doctor take her blood pressure and her temperature and write Mummy a prescription for her medication.

My family are Pentecostal Christians and we go to the New Testament Assembly church on Sundays. **If we are worried we say a prayer to God.** We also pray if we want to thank God for something. My Mummy and Nanny taught me to say The Lord's Prayer off by heart and the 23rd Psalms which starts with the verse: The Lord Is My Shepherd I shall not want.

That means that God is always looking after us and taking care of us no matter what.

My Mummy's cardiologists, Professor Timmis and Dr Weir, told her that the arteries that pump blood to her heart were blocked, so she had to have an operation.

I was scared again and thought my Mummy would definitely die this time. I cried when she was packing her suitcase for the hospital but she said that I should not be afraid. My Mummy told me that all people have to die at sometime but it was important that we are brave and remember the good things about that person and the happy times. When she had gone I asked God to make my mum get better so she could come home.

I did not want to think about a life without my Mummy.

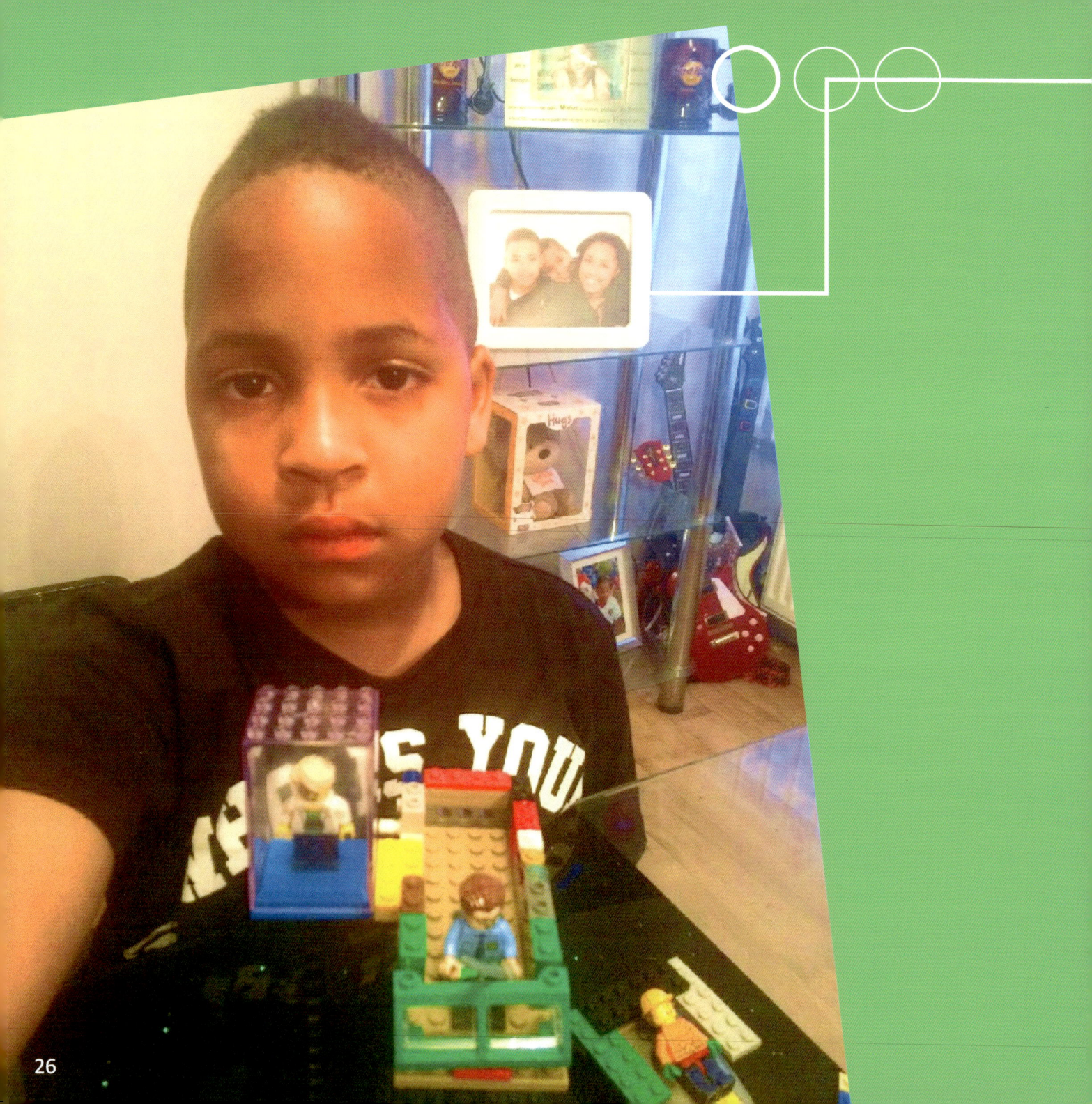

My family were always smiling and staying positive, and that would stop me from worrying about my Mummy being in hospital getting ready to have a serious operation.

I knew in my heart that God would look after her.

To help me forget what was happening, I would play with my Lego.

I felt scared of the dark and wanted my bedroom light to stay on at bedtime.

i didn't want to sleep by myself. I tried not to cry, even though I was missing my Mummy, and Nanny said I was very brave and strong. She told me that God would help the doctors to fix her heart, and that the nurses were taking good care of her.

I just wanted my Mummy to come home to look after me.

Mummy had heart bypass surgery at the London Chest Hospital in Bethnal Green. The surgeons had to put her to sleep, and took three arteries from her left leg and one from her chest.

When she came home, she had two long scars: one down the inside of her left leg and the other down the middle of her chest. She was in a lot of pain. Her feet were also very swollen, and couldn't fit into her shoes. I was just happy she was alive.

I would rub cocoa butter on her feet every day, because she could not bend down, and I helped to put on her compression stockings so she didn't get blood clots.

I remember one day when I came home from school, Mummy was crying because she was in a lot of pain. The scar on her chest was hurting her. I gave her a kiss and big hug to make her feel better.

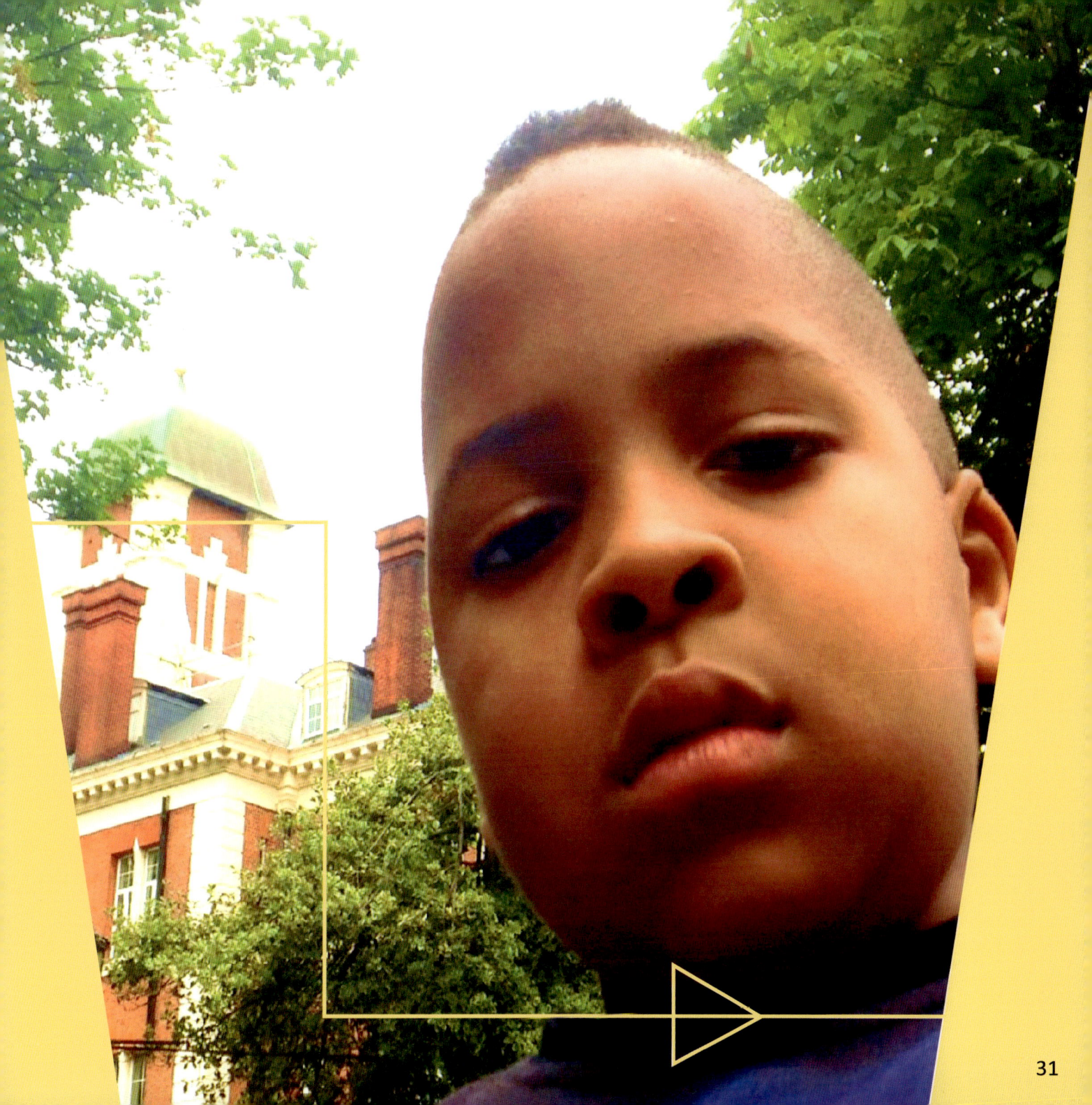

Every day my Mummy got stronger and stronger. I worked hard at school so mummy didn't have to worry about me.

after three months the pain in Mummy's chest had not got better but the swelling on her feet went down and her shoes finally fit. The Doctor said she had to walk every day and it was my job to make sure she remembered. Mummy wasn't strong enough to take K-9 for her walks in the park, so I would go with my sister.

Mum wants to raise money for the **British Heart Foundation** and we did a 5k run for the Charity.

We have also donated furniture and electrical items to one of their shops. I packed a bag with clothes that do not fit me anymore and have also donated two black bags filled with my toys so I can help to raise lots of money too.

I love my Mummy very much and even though I do not want to disappoint her I am going to have to be honest. I am not going to be a Cardiologist.

In fact, I'm not going to be a footballer or a Jedi either. I have decided, I am going to be an Architect and make fantastic buildings like the White House in Washington and the Eifel Tower in Paris. I know I will be successful and be able to create brilliant designs because I have had a lot of practice. **Last night I made Big Ben which is a massive clock tower in Westminster in London.** *I did this all by myself, at home with my Lego.*

Romeo and Tiverton's Focus Group Glossary

Hackney: A place in east London

Lego: Small plastic building blocks that you can use to make toy buildings and cars or just use your imagination.

Divorced: When your parents are not married any more.

Museums: A building that people visit to see lots of old and important things from history like dinosaurs.

Pantomimes: A play you watch at Christmas with songs and jokes.

Legoland: A theme park with fun rides and lots of Lego.

Star Wars: The best movie in the world.

Jedi: Superheroes in Star Wars that defeat the bad guys with their lightsabers.

Construction: When you build something.

Instructions: Tells you what to do, step by step.

Imagination: When you think about ideas using your mind.

Tottenham Hotspur Football Club: The best English football team in the Premier League (written by my Mummy).

Arsenal Football Club: A football team (written by my Mummy).

Senior Deputy Head Teacher: The second person in charge of a school.

Secondary School: The school you go to after primary school when you are 11.

Cardiologist: A special doctor who looks after your heart.

Architect: A person who designs and makes buildings.

Jamaica: An island in the Caribbean.

Cornmeal Porridge: Jamaican porridge that you have for breakfast.

Ackee and Saltfish: A famous Jamaican meal.

Pumpkin: A round orange Halloween vegetable.

Godmother: A person chosen by your parents who will take care of you if your parents die.

Heart Attack: What happens when the blood that flows to your heart gets blocked.

Discharged: When you can leave hospital.

Blood Pressure: A test to see if your blood is pressure is normal. It is dangerous if it is too high or too low.

Temperature: A test to see if your temperature is normal. It is dangerous if it is too high or too low.

Prescription: A sheet of paper you get from the doctor that tells you what medicine or tablets you need to get from the chemist.

Medication: Tablets or medicine.

Pentecostal Christians: Christians that believe in God and believe that you must be baptized if you are going to go to heaven.

Arteries: Small tubes in the body that carry blood from the heart to the rest of your body.

Bypass Surgery: An operation where you are given new arteries because some of yours are blocked.

Blood Clots: When your blood goes hard.

Surgical Stockings: Special socks that stop blood clots in your legs.

British Heart Foundation: A Heart Charity that raises money to try and stop people from dying from heart problems.

Donate: To give money or clothes to a good cause.

The White House: Where the President of the United States lives in Washington DC.

Eiffel Tower: A famous tall tower building in Paris, France.

Big Ben: The bell in the clock tower at the end of the Houses of Parliament in Westminster.

Westminster: A place in the centre of London.

Thank You

I want to thank God for looking after me and my family, especially my Mummy. Thank you to my sister Yazmin for helping me with the writing, my brother Bailey for printing my book, Andy Pryor, my Designer, Jackie Raymond my Editor, Tiverton Primary school for reading my draft and making very good comments, my Nanny Lilly, Uncle Kevin, Uncle Wayne, Aunty Lizzy, Uncle Mark, Aunty Julia, Aunty Joan, Uncle Tony, Aunty Carmen Campbell, Granddad Ken, Mama Gem, Uncle Peter McKenzie, Mr Tom, Miss Komer and all the teachers at St Paul's with St Michael's and all of my school friends. Thank you to Aunty Marcia Dixon, Aunty Juliet Fletcher, Aunty Jenny Irish, Aunty Odette Brooks, Aunty Glynis Glasgow, Aunty Dorothy Hall, Aunty Ade Adebambo, Aunty Hazel Graham, Aunty Louise Mangal, Aunty Jacqui O'Donnell, Aunty Denice Sealy, Aunty Paulette Long, Aunty Carleen Graham, Aunty Lanette Gayle, Raymond, Cassie and Keon Ismailah, Uncle Roland, Aunty Liz, all of my gazillion cousins, Marvin Campbell, Gary Williams, Jackie Hamilton and Jane from First Steps.

And my Mummy wants to thank Mr Hartney, Sam Lynch, Michael Lowe, Angela Jones, Mehreen Baig, Goldwater Ojokor, Engin Djemali, Andrew Aibangbee, Sonia Bardouille, Reggie Stober, Ijeaku Mezue, Maarya Desai, Filipe Vasconcelos, Arminda Di Vito, Pauline Jones, Lee Carryl, Tugcan Cankaya, Andy Jackson, Tameka Dublin, Gonce Avas, Subashani Naidoo, Sharon Nandal, Sophie Mtandwa, Seema Chandler, Ordella Fenton, Eileen Edwards, Samantha Pennells, Ty Lowe, Iyabo Agbelusi, Sharon Williams, Rob Porter, Caroline Brown, Christine Hayes, Cathy Burrill, Amanda Craig, Warren Reid, Ilhan Gozubuyuk, Antuneil Thompson, Camille Jean-Marie, Yiannis Demetriou, Caleb Oluwafemi, Godfrey Davis, Louiza Leon, Emma Davis, May Oduah, Julia Padmore, Adam Head, the sooper dooper English and Media Faculty and the rest of the Gladesmore family.

Thank You (continued)

Elizabeth Reilly, Jan Oztun Ali, Debra Robinson, Ros Griffiths, Nketci Hunter, Robert Rhoden, Angie Le Mar, Bonny Lockhart, Bryan Powell, Francis Florent, Frances Newell, Sarah Nichols, Carine Swaby, Rosemarie Muhammad, Undeane Barton, Sicsley Hillocks, Lillieth McLeod, Caroline Marsh, Fiona Murray, Pauline Burke, Sharon Graham, Donovan Hall, Annie Bartley, Pat and Kit Stanford, Shaquelle Green, Rick Mason and Carol Ricketts.

And all the people who helped her to get better: Dr Anna Pilkington and everyone at Queensbridge Group Practice, Professor Adam Timmis, Dr William Ian Weir, Dr Chris Efthymiou and everyone at the London Chest hospital. Sapan Sehgal from London Fields Fitness, the team from Cardiac Rehabilitation especially Maureen Barry and Thelma Adu, Nikki and Katarina from Britania's Healthwise, Shirley Coventry at St Leonards, Tracy at SW, Mother Payne, Sister Pearl Jones, Sister Carmen Leslie, Sister Grace Straker, Sister Ricketts, Sister Earla, Pastor Marjorie Esomowei, Bishop John and Penny Francis, Nicky Brown, Bishop Delroy Powell, Rev Richard Ade-Martins, the Wednesday Bible Study Group and all her NTA family.

**Special thanks to Headteacher Resham Mirza, Assistant Head Siobhan Barry and the staff and Year 2 students from Tiverton Primary school, N15, who took part in the research focus group:
Anry, Natty, Natali, Shakira, Theo, Tyler, Mahbub, Kaan, Clarissa, Kelvin, Emma, Valerio, Nasra, Rumaysa and Aya.**

Love Romeo x

I wrote this six months after the birth of my son, Romeo. It was supposed to encourage and support new mothers whose babies were born premature. I thought I'd share it with you.

My Prince in Egypt

No parent expects their child to die before them, so when my husband's eldest passed away at 22, with a brain haemorrhage on Father's Day 2006, the whole family was devastated.

A year on, at 42, I was shocked to discover I was pregnant with my third child. The whole family was excited at the prospect of a new addition, and we planned a family Christmas holiday to Tunisia in North Africa. I fell ill and was hospitalised at the beginning of the fortnight, and was diagnosed by the doctors as suffering from pneumonia. Even though I was twenty weeks pregnant, I was subjected to numerous x-rays; put on an intravenous drip; overloaded with medication, and my heart was regularly monitored. At one point it was touch and go, and I spent three days being closely monitored in isolation in intensive care.

After two weeks under close observation, it was agreed that I could go home and, on New Year's Eve, I was transported from the hospital to the airport and flown back to the UK, only to welcome in the New Year by being admitted straight to Queen's Hospital in Essex.

My condition deteriorated and, after extensive tests and a blood transfusion, it was revealed that not only did I have pneumonia, but I was also suffering from Crohn's disease, and would need to have a piece of my colon removed. In order for this to happen, my baby would have to be delivered by emergency caesarean - eight weeks early.

My little 2.43 kilogram miracle, Romeo, was born on 2nd March, Mother's Day 2008. Very weak and in intense pain, my first look at my son was eight hours after he was born, on a Polaroid taken by a kind nurse. He was smaller than my husband's palm, and spent the first weeks of his life in an incubator in Homerton Hospital's Neonatal Unit.

The operation for the Crohn's was postponed until I was stronger, and I had to stay in hospital to be monitored closely by the medical team. I was wheeled over to the Special Care Baby Unit (SCBU) daily, and the nurses fed, changed and cared for little Romeo in my absence.

He was nicknamed 'Prince Blessing' by the family, and my Prince grew stronger and stronger by the day. The wires that covered him were eventually removed, and he was given a daily dose of iron and vitamins.

Baby Romeo was finally discharged from hospital to the care of my mother and husband, while I waited in hospital for a decision on whether I was to be operated on.

Six weeks after his birth I was discharged, and spent the first night with my son. He would stiffen and cry when I held him, and the knowing glances and little coos were reserved for my mother and husband. It was clear that he had bonded with them, and what made things even more difficult was that included in my daily medication of 22 tablets were steroids, meaning breastfeeding was not an option.

I knew I had a lot of work to do and that it was going to take time, but that was not a problem - I had all the time in the world.

Twenty-four weeks on, and Prince Blessing is a cheeky, chubby six-month-old who smiles endlessly, laughs, chatters and loves to be kissed and cuddled. I am amazed at how strong he is, and how far he has come from his early days in Homerton's Special Care Baby Unit. Amazingly, those days are a distant memory.

When I look at my little miracle, I thank God for every day, every smile and every laugh.

Today, we are miles away from home, bonding on a beach in Sharm El-Sheikh, and I am reflecting on the journey my little Romeo has taken over the last six months. I'm still suffering from Crohn's, but I know I and my family are blessed.

As I look out into the Red Sea, I promise to enjoy every precious moment with my little miracle because, today, Prince Romeo is **My Prince in Egypt**.

Juliet Bremmer, August 2008

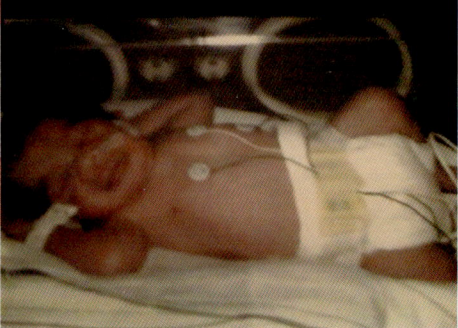